I0560518

To my Mom. Your courage and resilience is breathtaking.

Madness Heart Press
2006 Idlewilde Run Dr.
Austin, Texas 78744

This is a work of fiction. Names, characters, places, and incidents either are the product of the author's imagination or are used fictitiously. Any resemblance to actual persons, living or dead, events, or locales is entirely coincidental.

Copyright © 2025 Susan Snyder
Cover by Rooster Republic

All rights reserved. No part of this book may be reproduced or used in any manner without written permission of the copyright owner except for the use of quotations in a book review. For more information, address: john@madnessheart.press

First Edition
ISBN: 978-1-967517-02-2
www.madnessheart.press

Ten Words for a Wicked Woman

SUSAN SNYDER

A Madness Heart Press Publication

Table of Contents

Introduction

This book is NOT about me. Okay, yes, it is about me. But this isn't some ego-based memoir to toot my own horn or cultivate some type of fan base. I know what you're thinking.

Only an ego-based memoir writer who's trying to cultivate a fan base would say that.

Look, I have been through some shit. So has every other woman in the world. To varying degrees of horror. My purpose in this little book is to share my own experiences as one of the females of our species. Every single woman who reads this will relate to one or more of these experiences. It's a fact. A terrible reality.

This is also not a handbook of any sort. Do not, repeat DO NOT read this as advice. I fucked pretty much everything up.

We have entered, at the time of my finishing this book, a very strange circus of uncertainty. The rights of women are being stripped away, crumpled up and tossed into an awaiting rubbish bin. We women are frantically trying to retrieve them, smooth them out, write "Fuck You" in bubble letters, crumple it back up and shove it directly up a white man's tight little asshole.

It's getting rough.

Alright, maybe writing this was a catharsis for me. I had to look at some shit that I hadn't peered at directly...ever. I admit some things that are embarrassing, that may not paint me in the best light or feature my good side.

But I am being honest.

We need to speak up and speak out. Summon all our courage. Grab our crotches* and spit. Get tough. Pound our chests. Howl like banshees.

This little book is my rant against our march backward into patriarchy. It's a gander at hypocrisy and inner turmoil. There is mature language, sexual situations and smoking. My parents might disown me. People may poke fun at me for even trying to pull off a piece of work like this. But I write with self-deprecating humor, so I beat you to the punch, folks. Ha!

Of course, there is a possibility that this book just sucks and my little female fingers would have been of better use crocheting or inserting a tampon or wiping my tears. Ya know, regular woman stuff.

I shall let you be the judge. Go ahead and judge me. That's what I am here for. While you do, just keep one question in mind.

Why would she do that?

Therein, you may find some disturbing answers. If you are a woman, you probably already know the answers.

Let's dig into my pain, shall we?

*Please note that I said grab *our* crotches. Our own. Nobody else's crotches. Your individual crotch only please. And use *your own* hand to grab *your own* crotch. Nobody else's hand. Your own individual hand. Please.

Susan Snyder

Abandoned

I have kicked a lot of little elementary school boys in the dick. Granted, I too was in elementary school at the time. I don't want to give the impression that as a full grown woman I went around roundhousing young boys in the family jewels. I also don't want to give the impression that my youth made it okay. It was not my finest time in life.

In the moment when my little foot assaulted their little peckers, I truly saw nothing wrong with it. It also afforded me a reputation based on crippling fear, which I quite enjoyed. I even tried to recruit fellow females into my dick-kicking club, which didn't pan out. Imagine my disbelief when other little girls found my actions reprehensible. A teacher or two confronted me about my penal onslaught of terror on the playground fields. Eventually, I stopped.

In the dead of night, when my brain chooses to revisit painful memories instead of fucking sleeping, I often wonder if this set off a metaphysical karmic chain of events in my life where men enacted their collective revenge for my actions in fifth grade. Maybe these boys grew up to do untoward things to women as a result of the trauma I caused them. I might just be the psychological impetus for domestic violence or sexual assault. Probably not.

But maybe?

As you shall see as this book unfolds, I paid a hefty price. I would take it as personal directed vengeance for my transgressions in elementary school, except legions of other women have gone through similar, or much worse, experiences in their lifetimes. Did they all kick dicks as a child? The answer is, again, probably not. It seems I was a rare specimen of a girl who looked at the males of my species as the enemy. That's not rare per se. But booting innocent boys in the jimmy is kind of rare.

In addition to my grade school tirade of genital violence, I was a pathological liar. Being a gifted youth, having skipped second grade for my academic acumen, I learned how to use my intelligence to manipulate people and situations to devise my chosen outcome. A budding sociopath that would eventually grow out of it, a decade later, I have since channeled this into intense self-hatred and the writing of extreme horror stories. You're welcome, society.

I would skip homework or projects and fabricate intricate stories of excuses and situations beyond my control. The school counselor called my mom in to discuss my behavior. I never really got in trouble. They felt bad for me because of the divorce and all. I may have dialed the fibbing down as I got into my teens but I pulled out my old tricks when backed into a corner. If I thought a rule or an assignment or a feeble attempt at parental control had any cracks in the facade, I would slip right through that crevasse like a lubricated cockroach.

What was the genesis of all this devious shit? My dad abandoned me.

Would my father agree that he abandoned his only child at the supple age of six? In my adulthood, I came to realize that he was most likely going through some of his own shit, untangling his own double knots that life loves to shove down your throat like a non-consensual ball-gag. But this is written and interpreted by *my* brain. This is my point of view on it. This is how I honestly felt at the time and for a long time after.

Boy, did this have a lifelong effect on my relationships with men.

The one man I loved, and thought loved me, left me. I was a daddy's girl through and through. We were attached at the hip pre-divorce. He was my goddamn hero. We wrote books together, him assisting me with my creation as he wrote down and illustrated unknown classics such as *Seymour, the Hungry Seal* and *The Little Schoolhouse That Wanted to Grow.* It was just for us. Our thing. He encouraged my fledgling love of sharks, which became my life's passion later on. We geeked out about dinosaurs.

When you're young, you have no fucking clue about your parents' relationship. They are just always there. You take it for granted if you are lucky enough to have both parents and are in a safe and stable environment. I was a cute little white girl living in Southern California. Semi-spoiled and well behaved. I say this not to rub it into the faces of anyone who had a difficult upbringing. I say this to show that, despite variations in socioeconomic status, divorce can fuck up kids just the same.

My recollections of events surrounding the divorce are fuzzy at best. My dad was there and then he was not. Once, I caught my mom crying at the top of the stairs. She would drop vague disparaging remarks about my dad. I would visit with my dad in another place, another separate home. He would spew unflattering lines about my mom. Things were no longer in order. A disturbance in the Force.

Since I was the one volleying back and forth between my separated parents like a partially deflated beach ball, this was all clearly my fault.

Then came my own swift kick to the balls. My dad took up with another family. He ended up marrying a woman who had two of her own children. His priority shifted over to them. I was no longer the center of my father's universe. When my dad had visitation, I had to endure getting to know these alien invaders. They seemed nice enough at first. Over time, the two girls roped me into shoplifting, and we got busted. Funny how they stuffed the candy bars down *my* pants. When confronted by authorities, they threw their hands up in unison, declaring me the criminal mastermind. Innocuous now, but at the time, it was a big deal. Another time, I was shipped off with those girls to some Bible retreat thing hosted by evangelists who sang dopey songs about how Christ loves us, and who appeased the masses with large amounts of cheap candy. The "stepmom" figure who took away my father's affections turned out to have a rumored history of prostitution (not sure if that is true and I don't really care if it was). The girls allegedly grew up to be junkies and/or Jesus freaks (also not sure if true, but it tracks).

I was gobsmacked that my dad chose these lunatics over me. *ME!* His actual kid.

Meanwhile, at home, my mom did her best to keep things going. We made fast friends with the neighbors in our apartment complex. They were from Trinidad and Tobago and their place always smelled so fascinating, with exotic aromatics wafting out of pots simmering on the stove. They were part of a steel drum band at San Diego Wild Animal Park (now called Safari Park). On the stage, they were joined by traditional and limbo dancers from Africa, and they too became close friends. We went to this zoo a lot. I even graced the stage once and limboed with Janet, the crowd delighting at this little white weirdo grooving with the performers. I wasn't wanting to replace my dad by any means, but I fell in love with a member of the band and tried to convince my mother to marry him. She wasn't totally opposed to it either. This guy was a cutie patootie. These people were wonderful and that is all I cared about. I guess this matchmaking phase meant I was healing. Who knows? It didn't last.

Eventually, my mom needed help raising a kid on her own. We moved out to Massachusetts to live with my grandparents. My dad and his new family lived in Colorado. I flew out there to see him one time and it was super awkward. He tried, he really tried to be a dad to me, but the luster had left the rose. I could feel the disconnection. By this time, I was about eleven or twelve and had grown accustomed to life without him. I had dick-kicked and lied my way through some of the anger I felt from him abandoning me.

My mom and dad did not have a co-parenting situation. They hated each other. My father owed tons of back child support, and over time -- which to me seemed overnight -- he stopped contacting me. The lines went dead. Daddy had left the building.

That's when the fun really started. I transformed into hell on wheels. I'll talk more about that in another section, but suffice to say, I was incorrigible.

This whole dynamic metamorphised in my mind into rejection by my dad, by a man, and thus by *all* men. When I reached age fourteen, now bleeding monthly and pubescent as holy hell, my twisted frontal lobe decided that the best way for me to regain the love and affection of men was sex. That's what men want, right? By golly, if sex is what they want, then surely I will provide this for them. After all, sex means love. Sex isn't complicated or risky at all. Eureka! I shall be loved by all men!

As is the case with my horrible teenage behavior, my promiscuity will be discussed at length elsewhere. They are both misplaced reactions to the anger of my parent's divorce. There were no siblings or even childhood friends to turn to. Any friends I had in California were gone once I was relocated over to the East Coast. Living at my Nana and Grampy's gorgeous affluent home in a suburb south of Boston, I was in a neighborhood full of kids my age. Rich kids. To the naked eye, living in a huge home on the corner of a very fru-fru area, I must also be rich and from a healthy nuclear family structure.

My grandparents' home had four bedrooms and a huge furnished basement. My Uncle George (the *good* uncle, not the creepy uncle) lived in one of those bedrooms, my grandparents had the master and my mother and I shared one of the two remaining bedrooms. *Shared the bedroom.* We slept in the same bed. Mind you, there was another unoccupied bedroom next door. I was discouraged from going in there, let alone having my own room. Same with the carpeted, comfortable basement. No, I had to sleep with my fucking mom.

The basement became my sanctuary, though. I couldn't sleep down there, and truth be told, it was a very creepy place at night, but I spent most of my free time in that basement. I recorded myself with my boom box and blank cassette tapes. Like a bastardized fledgling Weird Al, I parodied lyrics to popular songs. I mimicked news reporters. I roped my Uncle George and his girlfriend CarolAnn, who were both in their very early twenties, to join me for recorded interviews and fart jokes while they were high as balls on weed.

The neighborhood kids, who I also went to school with, took notice of my inexpensive clothes and strict curfews, and it was collectively decided that I was white trash posing as upper-middle class. A few of them stuck by me, but a good chunk of these kids had called out my bullshit. I can only imagine the hardship I wreaked upon my mother as I relentlessly begged her for a Gucci pocketbook or designer jeans. She obliged me as much as she could. Even my extended family went all out for Christmas and showered me with more presents than any one child should ever receive. The elusive Cabbage Patch Kid, the Atari 2400 gaming system (and every other new gaming system as the years progressed), tons of nice clothes and shoes, countless cassettes of pop stars. Looking back, it boggles my brain. Total annihilation of guilt by overcompensation.

It was not a good idea to spoil a kid who has sociopathic tendencies and abandonment issues. Once puberty kicked in, I was in a feeding frenzy and about to bite some folks in their unsuspecting asses. Well, mostly my mom's ass.

When I was about sixteen years of age, my dad reappeared quite unexpectedly. He called and spoke with my mom for a bit. When I got on the phone, we had a nice catch up. He told me that he was nearly killed in a car wreck and spent a lot of time being put back together in the hospital. By this time, his other family was history. My guess is that his close call with death forced him to take stock of his life, of the fact that he had one kid out there and had had little to nothing to do with her for nearly a decade. He came out to visit and bought me my first car. He and my mom seemed to tolerate each other. We kept in touch over the phone and eventually became close again. I lived with him in Houston for a while when I got older. He financed a lot of world travels that we embarked on together: South Africa, Thailand, Costa Rica, Mexico, Alaska, and tons of road trips. He gave me a lot of money when I'd call him with my hand out. Dang, I'm fifty years old now and he *still* helps me out when I need it, albeit more begrudgingly since I should probably have my shit together by now.

So my father and I are now besties. All is forgiven, right?

Yes and no.

Like I said, I have come to realize that he didn't maliciously set out to throw me aside like yesterday's chopped liver. But the damage is done. It cannot be reversed. The rippling effect of my desperation for a man's love and my insatiable anger toward my very existence took its toll on me. It got me into circumstances that were downright dangerous. It pushed me to walk a razor's edge of mental fragility, of depression and anxiety, of sexual and domestic violence. I honestly don't know what life would have been like if my mom and dad stayed together. Or if they still split up but my dad stayed in my life during that decade of prime childhood real estate.

I can't blame my dad. I made my own choices. I made a bed of cocks and craziness and I was obligated to lie in it.

But could things have been different? Would life have been any better, easier, fruitful? Look, I currently own and lease a gaggle of problems. Sorting out which problems would have been avoided and which new problems would have reared their ugly heads is not only impossible, it doesn't sound fun. I have navigated the hand that I was dealt for fifty fucking years.

The devil you know is better than the devil you don't.

Cursed

I wrote a short story once about an underground Kaiju that feeds off the menstrual blood of women. My relationship with my reproductive organs may not be at the pussy-licking Kaiju level of awful, but it's close.

One thing you should never ever say to a young girl who just started her monthly visits from Aunt Flo is, "You're a woman now!"

The first reason being that she is not in any mood to celebrate. This is the first time blood is coming out of her yahoo, combined with strange feelings of ennui and terror. Maybe there is some pain from cramps. Even if she is one of the lucky ones who have had all this explained to her by a parent or whoever, this totally sucks. And if she had no idea this was coming, take a moment to think about that opening scene from *Carrie* when she gets sucker punched by her first period in the school locker room shower. It's that horrifying.

Another reason to refrain from that stupid saying is that you have just associated this atrocity with womanhood. I am not saying that womanhood is not an atrocity. It is. In so many ways. What you are saying here is, "Welcome to the shit show! Let the pain, trauma, sexual harassment, bullying, fear, panic and total dismissal of your feelings begin! And by the way, you also have to endure this crap each month unless you do something drastic like get a hysterectomy or get knocked up or have a doctor prescribe some birth control that will only postpone the fuckery! No matter what you do, you're completely fucked. Hooray! You're a woman now!" How any woman could say it like it's a *good thing* is a mystery to me. Not to mention, it is untrue and misleading. Womanhood is most definitely not a "yay!" situation.

The proper response should just be, "You got your period? You're fucked."

Yet, more than one of my family members, including my creepy uncle (EW!) said the other to me when I began on my ghastly path at the age of thirteen. My mom educated me on it. I had my starter kit of mini pads ready to go. Yet, when I came home from school and found this little bit of blood on my underwear, I almost puked. Perhaps it was foresight into what would become a lifetime of misery which all would emanate from or be related to my reproductive organs. I felt the oncoming red tide of bullshit. I sensed the probing, hungry tongue of the Kaiju that would follow me like a monstrous overbearing shadow.

So, yah. Don't fucking say that to a girl who just started her cycle. Or if you do, allow the young lady to tell you to "fuck off" without any repercussions.

The simple fact is that women have always been treated differently since time immemorial because of our reproductive system. It rules our lives and determines our fate. Some women have it easier than others. I am one of the chosen ones, the blood warriors, the pussy patriots, who have had to endure biological trials of pain and suffering for our entire lives.

I'm so lucky, so blessed. It has made me stronger and resilient. It has shown me that my strength is... just kidding! It is a diabolical infernal life of living hell.

I am not sure when my uterus turned against me but I would guess it was around the age of fifteen. My cramps were progressively getting worse. Once, in college, I collapsed on the floor in the co-ed bathroom, hyperventilating from the torment in my loins. The RA called an ambulance and I was rushed to the emergency room. They gave me a whopping shot of some pain medication and left me there to rot alone.

Fun fact: I am incredibly tolerant of pain medication. Meaning, it don't work on me.

After like two hours, someone returned to find me still writhing in agony. Into my buttocks went another shot of something or other. Finally, it settled me down. The diagnosis? Stomach cramps. Um. Did you skip the fact that I was on my period?

This was the first notable time that a physician disregarded my complaint about my womanly body parts. But it wasn't the last. My entire life was permeated, and still is, by "doctors" both male and female, who barely listen or register any need to dig into the cause of pain and misery related to being a woman with organs and hormones that rule her life like a dark menses overlord.

At the age of sixteen, I went on birth control pills as a futile attempt to curb my cramps. It did help with cramps. But it made me completely bat shit crazy. And I did not need any help in that department, thank you very much. I had plenty of mental muddle of my own making.

I suppose I'm grateful that the birth control part of those pills kept me from getting pregnant. No child wants to be brought into this world with me as a mother. Plus, the already formidable foe that is my lower abdomen would have most likely killed me in the process anyway.

You may not know this, but a lot of the things that might cause severe pain and distress for women cannot be easily diagnosed by orthodox means. Endometriosis, pelvic inflammatory disease, ruptured ovarian cysts and uterine fibroids are all mainly soft tissue maladies. They don't show up on X-rays. You need ultrasounds, and even then, you better hit that at just the right time. I had many cysts on my ovaries rupture. This was undoubtedly what happened in college. But by the time a competent doctor would even manage to take a peek with an ultrasound, which most would never even do, the cyst has already ruptured. Gone. Nothing to see. Cue doctor shrugging condescendingly and dismissing you.

Later in life, in my forties, a gynecologist finally got the idea to look for uterine fibroids. This was after decades of waves of "Holy hell! What the actual fuck?" torture at various times on the spectrum of my cycles. Pain that would go hand in glove with vomiting, extreme mood swings, missing work, thoughts of suicide, massive doses of ibuprofen and curling up in a fetal position enduring aches akin to full fledged labor pains. Decades of this. All the time. Always dismissed by doctors. All the fucking time.

Boy howdy did I have a couple doozy fibroids. So this gyno convinced me to do a procedure called a uterine fibroid embolization (UFE). The doc would thread a tube up my artery and block the blood flow to my uterus using little micro plastics, thus depriving these womb gremlins of their nourishment. As is protocol, I informed the nurses that anesthesia didn't work on me. They didn't believe me. In the middle of the procedure, as I was intensely watching the monitor in awe of the miracle of modern medicine, I commented on how interesting it was to see what the surgeon was doing on the screen. The surgeon popped his head around the privacy curtain. "Wait! You are awake?" I responded affirmatively, to which he replied, "You're about to feel some stuff." And indeed I did.

Three post-surgery pain shots and a dose of Oxy later, I finally stopped screaming and puking long enough to get taken home. I went through a couple weeks of distress and, voila! The fibroids were almost completely unaffected by the whole damn thing. To this day, I still have them and, although they have not grown much, they haven't shrunken up in their despair over a lack of blood supply.

Gee, so glad I put myself through that.

The next thing that was suggested to me to "cure" (read: shut me up about) my ailments was to get quarterly injections of Depo Provera, a progesterone based form of birth control. I was told this too would allegedly help with fibroids and might even stop my periods altogether. I was right smack in the throes of a period when I got the first shot. Bammo! The period stopped and didn't return. I only had two injections. A single year's worth of this shit. What I wasn't told was that older women run a risk of bone loss while on this crap. I also wasn't told about the risk of stroke. So I quit the injections.

Got another shocker when researching and found out that it could take up to 18 months for progesterone levels to return to normal. It could cause early menopause. Nobody knows and everyone reacts differently. I prayed to my Dark Lord for menopause and thought my incantations were answered when I failed to have a period for another year! Huzzah! Maybe this lifelong ordeal caused by my extraneous and unuseful internal lady parts had finally come to an end! Oh the sweet sweet siren call of old age! I embrace you and do not give one single fuck that I am only fifty years old. Gimme the mustache, the sagging neck, the front porch rocking chair, the badly fitting dentures, the incontinence diapers. I don't care. Just make the pain stop.

I am a silly fool who briefly thought this might actually happen. I guess I kicked one too many dicks as a kid and so karma had other plans.

In March of 2024, I was still drinking three or four times a week. Still smoking ciggies. Rocking that sexy sedentary lifestyle. Ya know, not the epitome of pure health. So when I started to get tingling and numbness on the left side of my face, I thought, "Shit. Am I having a stroke?" I went to see a doctor, who thought, "Shit. Is she having a stroke?" I was sent over to the emergency room, where they thought, "Shit. She must be having a stroke!"

I was admitted to the hospital and put through the gamut of all the imaging and probing that is standard for stroke protocol. They found nada. Zilch. Again, I was dismissed by a doctor who simply shrugged me off and suggested maybe it was just stress or migraines. I got in to see my primary care doc and she had no clue. Insert mandatory shrug. I got referred to an Ear, Nose and Throat specialist because I began having severe vertigo as well. Shruggy shrug shrug. Must be stress. After waiting six fucking months to see a neurologist, I got a hearty and very shruggy "Beats me! Must be stress!" All the while, I was telling them about the fact that I was probably in menopause or about to be and wouldn't it maybe have something to do with my fluctuating hormones and couldn't it… "Shut the fuck up and heed my shrug, you filthy idiot!"

Currently, I am perimenopausal and my monthly friend visits every two weeks. Yep. It comes *more often* now. The last one was accompanied by some of the most debilitating pain I had had in years. And it IS all due to hormones. How do I know? It certainly didn't come from an expected source. My chiropractor and his wife helped me to get onto supplements designed for this particular travesty that alleviated a lot of the most mind-fucking symptoms. A goddamn chiropractor. But the main point is that I stumbled upon a man with medical knowledge and a menopausal wife. However I got here, I'm grateful I did.

The last chapter will explore the deep recesses of my aging pussy and all her surrounding peers. If you feel like focusing more on my vagina in her more lusty and tantalizing years, go ahead and skip over to the "Slut" section of the book.

I won't judge you for that. I'll just shrug.

You are all DISMISSED!

Susan Snyder

Mother

One of the greatest boo-boos in Mother Nature's design is the lack of an "off" button for a women's reproductive system. Should we decide to forgo that whole motherhood thing, too bad. You must still suffer the cycle. The cycle that is entirely mapped out to conceive, incubate and birth a child. Gotta do it, sisters. Suck it up.

Should you veer off into the breeding group and have a family, best cross all your digits that it doesn't come out a girl. Why? Because she will face an uphill slog of epic proportions just being a fucking woman.

Want to have a hysterectomy or tubal ligation to keep from even getting pregnant? Good luck finding a doctor that will do it. Most will pound your face with lamentations of "You'll change your mind," and "You're too young to make that decision."

Because, folks, the *purpose*, the very *existence* of

a woman is all about birthin' them babies. Old white men say so, and since they rule the world, it must be true. It's also backed up by a millennium of bastardized religious texts thumped and waved akimbo by said white men and their subservient wives, these women being either brainwashed, abused or lacking a functioning cell in their brain.

I've never been pregnant. I am surprised as you are that I came out of life unscathed by a searching little semen swimmer, especially given the amount of sex I've had in my fertile years. I am lucky. *VERY lucky*. My fragile mental health would not be able to handle the shit storm I would have to weather if I did. You see, I am of the ilk that believes a woman has *gasp* inherent worth as a human being regardless of her production of offspring. I never wanted kids. Ever. That decision came about at a very young age and I stuck with it. Two decisions actually: no kids, no marriage. Stuck with both of them.

I know, right? What a rebel. What a punk. I have the brass cojones to think I might matter anyway, having no brood and no man to overwrite my last name. What good am I?

In addition to our supporting roles as creator and caretaker, women are also here to serve as sexual pleasure vessels. A feast for the eyes and the flesh alike. Our consent is not required and would likely be reimagined as consent anyway in the heat of the moment, or when finding oneself the subject of a barroom brag. Do all men rape? Of course not. Are men also raped? You're damn right they are. But let's be real and shoot straight here. The vast majority of sexual violence and exploitation are perpetrated against women by men. This is a non-negotiable fact. Don't disagree with me. Or, if you do, fuck you because I will tell everyone you said "yes" anyway.

Sucks, don't it?

I want to give you a prime example of a woman being treated like men's plaything. One woman's story. Just one woman in a multitude of women. Surely, this woman is the only one this ever happened to and is an anomaly. Wouldn't want to make anyone uncomfortable.

She was a gorgeous teenager. Old Hollywood looks with an innocence in her eyes. This was the sixties when everyone dressed in their Sunday best to chain smoke in airplanes. This girl goes to a party on Fire Island, which was, at that time, not the gay mecca that it is now. Sixties, remember?

You might also recall the term "slipping a mickey" was used then to describe when someone was "slipping a roofie." That hasn't changed much, I guess. Men are still slipping women stuff to incapacitate them so they can get it on with her impaired and unwilling orifice(s). So that happened to this girl and she was indeed victimized by a young man while she was unconscious. She awoke and overheard this prick bragging about it to his friends. Picking up a kitchen knife, she confronted him. It may not have hurt him or even forced him to reevaluate his raping ways, but let's hope that he at least peed himself a little.

From this rape, she got pregnant. Despite what Rep. Todd Akins thinks, a political twat who got publicly corrected in 2015 for using 13th century logic, women can and do often get impregnated by their assailants. So picture a sexually assaulted teenage girl in the sixties who finds herself pregnant in a time when you simply did not speak about such things, let alone report it to authorities, or sprout any thoughts of terminating the pregnancy. At best, the baby gets born and adopted by some barren couple from the 'burbs.

That hasn't changed much either, given that in 2024, states are prosecuting women for having fucking *miscarriages*. Fetus worship abounds now as it did then. Life of the fully formed and functional woman be damned! It's all about the speck of tissue with no neuroconnections to a brain or developed vital organs. All hail the fetus!

This was a good Catholic girl from a good family of six siblings. Inseminated by a sexual predator. What was she to do?

Well, she was dropped off somewhere to be picked up by strangers who whisked her off to a clandestine farmhouse where a veterinarian performed an abortion on her. Doesn't that sound delightful?

This same girl was being visited at night by her creepy older brother. At home. In what was supposed to be her safe space, her sanctuary. He not only stalked her in the night, he did it to her sister while she had a friend sleeping over. I can personally attest that this guy was indeed prone to inappropriate behavior. Snapping my bra, patting my butt or making me sit on his lap when I was twelve years old.

This was in our family. Yah, this all happened to my mother.

Truth be told, when I was around the age my mother was when she was raped, I despised her. I knew nothing about her traumas. All I knew was that she was the person trying to keep me from doing everything and anything my teenage ass wanted to do, no matter how stupid and ill conceived it may have been. She was a bit of a cold fish as well. Not someone who expressed love or affection easily. She had a horrible spending problem. Long since divorced from my father, her choice of the rare male suitor was unpopular with me and her sisters.

Also, she ended up having one child who happened to be a grade-A horrid cunt of a daughter. Many teenagers act out, but not quite to the level I had. I'd say I hated my mother, but it was misplaced rage at the lack of a father figure, and no one was enforcing any real discipline on me. My mom was understandably overwhelmed. I plowed over her like a steamroller. If she told me "no" I would perform feats of harassment like calling her nonstop at work, physically attacking her, running away with some guy I barely knew, et al. One time, she retaliated by hitting me with a trash can. Good for her. I very much deserved it.

I was hanging out with metalheads and musicians. I thought that would piss her off but she quite liked my friends. I brought randoms over to stay at the house a few times. That'll get her going! No, she generously helped them out. Sometimes that was to a fault.

I blasted Metallica, especially the song *Dyers Eve*, from my bedroom often. For those not familiar, the lyrics are a thrashy rant against the failures of parents and society. Ha! That will get her! Nope. I caught her listening to one of my Metallica albums while she was cleaning one day.

I was smart. Still am. Really smart. Very manipulative. I've often wondered if I am a sociopath, but since I have mended my nefarious ways as life dragged on, as well as expressed authentic empathy for people, friends have told me I am not. The fascination with serial killers and death, all things morbid, is not because I *am* a serial killer. I just want to understand how they work.

Okay, so we've determined that I am not a psychopath. I had a mom who let me walk all over her like a doormat and dug longhaired dudes and heavy metal. I truly had a pretty cool mom. Yet, the resentment for her burned uncontrolled and hot in the dry shrubbery of my heart space.

Having sworn off bearing any children, and being so young, my empathy towards motherhood was severely lacking. In retrospect, I feel for my mother. Here was her only child, fruit of her loins, flesh of her flesh, who incessantly poked at her psyche on a daily basis. I could turn around and blame my parents for creating a monster. since their genetics composed my being. That's so easy to do, isn't it? "I never asked to be born!" That is a shallow redirection of responsibility. There are some horrible parents out there, and there are some horrible genetic predispositions that can be passed along to offspring. I stand alone, of my own free will. Despite any pre-programmed mental garbage that came along with me out of the birth canal, I knew what I was doing. I just didn't give a shit.

She divulged the rape to me when I was sixteen-ish. We were watching the movie *The Accused*, starring Jodie Foster as a woman gang-raped on a pool table in a bar. It's a true story that happened not too far away from where we lived in Massachusetts. She didn't know, nor did I tell her, that I had been the victim of some sexual assaults myself by that time. The movie was emotional for both of us but neither knew why the other was so blubbery. Then out it came. She casually mentioned her rape. I don't recall if I said anything to her in condolence or support. All I remember are the slippers she wore on her feet. That's it. Her slippers. They walked out of the room and into the kitchen, or maybe the bathroom, and I watched them as they moved.

I remember the intense hatred I had for my mom walking out of the room with those slippers. I mean, I was still a troublemaking douchecanoe until I was about eighteen. But now, I had a camaraderie of pain with my mother. A shared trauma bond. Much later, I would come to the conclusion that I shared that bond with almost every single fucking woman on the planet. Yet, there, on that night, it was the first time I *heard* another woman tell her tale. The rest of the story, as well as the revelation of her night-stalking brother, came out many many years later and in bits and pieces.

I feel terrible for how I treated my mom back then. I have apologized and repented. I now speak with her every couple days and we have grown close over the years. My mother is truly one of my heroes and one of the most open-minded people, accepting of all types without judgment. That woman made it through some scary shit, raised me by herself and maintained her sanity throughout. We always laugh when we're together. She puts up with my bullshit.

I just can't wrap my head around how some guy, let alone her own brother, could do those things they did to my mom. Then I expand outward, and outward, and outward. Isn't every woman who's trafficked, assaulted, raped, stalked and/

or murdered someone's mom, sister, daughter, whatever?

So the moral of this story is that women are here for the pleasure of men and the procreation of mankind. Old white men, who were rambunctious young men in the 1960's, make laws and say it's true. They would never inflict violence of this sort, nor would they have done so in the sixties at a party on Fire Island. Don't even *think* that. Just keep your focus on the fetus. The sweet sweet fetus.

And try not to be a dick to your mom.

Susan Snyder

Blasphemy

As I waited in line to accept the "body of Christ" into my mouth, as is protocol during the sacrament known as Confirmation, I was overcome with joy. With the exception of any funerals or weddings, this was the *last* time I would ever be in a church. Maybe it wasn't the joy that the awaiting priest at the end of the line expected, but joy nonetheless.

It was my turn and I strode up to this man of God, a visiting Bishop or Cardinal if I recall correctly, gaping my maw to receive the tasteless and dry wafer. My hands were demurely cupped in front of me just in case he decided to go the more polite route and place the thing there. Alas, like so many before and since, a man jammed something into my mouth before I knew what hit me. Not only that, he recoiled his hand like he had seen a spider pop out from behind my uvula and wink at him. Most would think this a bit rude. Not me. I smirked at him in bemusement. I had won the battle.

My presented hands were adorned with rings depicting demons, skulls and bats. Black as night were my fingernails. He may have missed the irony of my Ozzy Osbourne *Blizzard of Ozz* T-shirt that poked out above the vee neck of my Confirmation gown, the "Prince of Darkness" wielding a cross with a maniacal look on his face. But the silver pentagram pendant dangling from my neck was not missed. He saw that.

So. Much. Joy.

There was a time when I played with the idea of an actual, existing God and Satan. It didn't stick. When my mother moved us out to the East Coast, we resided with her parents. Part of the deal was that I attended the Catholic church at the end of the street. I didn't agree to that. But since when do children ever have a say-so in the plot points of their lives? Before we moved there, my mom didn't seem to give a rat's ass about going to church. In fact, I was behind in my education and development as a good, God-fearing American woman. When I got out to Massachusetts, I had to go to catch up private Bible classes with a nun and priest so that I could receive my First Communion in a timely manner, another hoop of a sacrament one has to jump through in order for God to save them or some shit.

For a fleeting moment, as Father Williams or Sister Catherine regaled me with fascinating tales of infanticide, treachery and violent persecution from the Good Book, I thought it might actually be true. Maybe, just maybe, there was a God and I better get my act together lest I be smote to the boiling pits of Hell. I even donned the goofy white dress and veil and had my First Communion solo in the middle of a regular Sunday mass. I was mortified.

It didn't end there. I had to get all the way through Confirmation before I would be allowed to think for myself as to whether or not I would continue with this. Apparently, that would signal my official understanding and wisdom and strengthen my bond with the church.

Well, I went a different way with that.

I was in a Youth Group, where teenagers are further indoctrinated into becoming Catholic automatons in anticipation that they will stick around after Confirmation. More sadistic Bible passages and once, a PG rated movie was shown about a neurotic young woman brainwashed into an unwanted pregnancy. Starring Molly Ringwald. I was still on the lure, not quite caught and hauled in, but not yet off the hook and swimming away. Sure I dressed up like Axl Rose for the Halloween party, but I wasn't questioning the validity of the entire religion.

Yet.

When they got into the Immaculate Conception, however, they lost me. Look, I may have been a young teenager who only dabbled in the dirty deed, but I knew where babies came from. I could smell a line of bullshit from a mile, being quite adept at producing it myself. So if I couldn't buy that a holy spirit angelically ethereal-raped Mary into birthing the son of God, then truly, the entire thing lost its footing.

I wanted Satan to be real. Oh, I yearned for it. Yet you can't believe in one and not the other, so my Devil dreams were dashed lest I be a self-judged goth hypocrite. The iconography of Old Scratch, though? I was *never letting go*. It was love at first sight. Horror books and movies, heavy metal music, anything black, pentagrams; you know the story. Long before I walked up to that Bishop and mocked the Eucharist, I was a bit obsessed with the idea of The Prince of Darkness (the non-Ozzy one).

He scares people. Makes them feel uncomfortable. From an early age I thrived on being a misfit, a rebel. The Devil was more of an aspiration than an abomination. I, too, loved making folks squirm. The seeds for my future extreme horror writing had been planted. My fervent adoration for all things horror and macabre had begun. It wasn't until much later that I realized what being a modern Satanist truly was.

In the beginning, Satan was the ultimate control freak hero to me. Ain't no one, no how, gonna tell the Dark One how to live, how to speak, how to dress, what to believe. Lucifer was the antithesis of my church's dogma of insanity: the twisted definition of gender roles, the conservative view of keeping everyone in line.

Then the Archdiocese of Boston got busted for molesting children.

Now, a naive little Susan thought that being exposed as not only perpetrating, but covering up, some of the most heinous crimes one can ever commit might be the downfall of the Catholic Church. Nope. My family didn't seem to blink. I don't remember anyone really speaking about it other than the talking heads on the nightly news. For fuck's sake, priests raped children! Yet, the church remained, and as time would reveal, the abuse continued.

My friend stole a copy of Anton Lavey's *The Satanic Bible* for me when I was about sixteen. It was around the time of the Confirmation. I was downright giddy to read this guidebook to the ultimate in murder and mayhem. Color me baffled when I realized almost everything in it *made sense*. It was a treatise on allowing humans to be humans. It was a diatribe on how if God made us in his own image, why did he set the rules in opposition to our natural instincts and dispositions? Indulgence and righteous revenge. Lust and protestation. I would be lying if I said I wasn't a teensy bit disappointed at the lack of cannibalistic hordes consuming aborted fetuses. I mean, after all, we had just endured the "Satanic Panic," and according to talk show moron Geraldo, these derelicts were legion and coming after our babies, born and unborn. The morbid curiosity within me was not at all satisfied. I expected the *Necronomicon* and got Martha Stewart's *Cookbook of Living Logically*. Fuck, the Bible classes were more grotesque than *The Satanic Bible*. By a long shot.

The only "Satanist" I ever met in real life was a weirdo semi-stalker of mine who had six fingers on each hand. I barely knew the guy and I'll be damned if I can remember his name. He found out where I lived and left a postcard with Satan on one side and the message "Smile for a while, girl-woman!" in my mail slot. I remember that message because I was freaked out. I had a Devil worshiper leaving me cryptic notes written by his hands with too many fingers. I was such a fucking stuck up bitch at the time that I felt truly indignant. Offended. That poor harmless guy was just trying to flirt with me and I made sure to scream from the rooftops about how my life was surely in danger from the six-fingered Satanist! Whatever made me the center of attention, I guess. Deep down in my soul, I admired the guy for being so open as a follower of the Lord of the Flies.

I was such an asshole.

Another thing that accurately describes me is the term "Truth-Seeker." Maybe I found this whole Satanism thing a bit boring once I knew what it was really all about. I was too young and lacking experience to realize the deep and profound resonance of that religion. And it *is* a religion. That word still reeked of establishment and indoctrination for me. If this wasn't my chosen path, then there had to be one more fitting out there somewhere.

Cue the circus parade of spiritual practices both witchy and woo woo.

Wicca? Check.

Divination? Check.

Staring at a scrying mirror for no good reason? Check.

Transcendental meditation? Check.

Yoga? Check.

Hindu cults? Check. (More on that in the Covens section).

This permeated my entire life. I never mastered any practice. Just dabbled in varying degrees until I got bored when big dicks and bars of gold failed to rain down upon me. I was looking for the answer to the *why* of it all. Sure, we all want to know the fucking point of our existence. But more crucially, I wanted to know the *how*. How to make money. How to get that guy. How to be adored by millions. How to not burn toast. How to navigate among the unwashed masses. How to survive. How to process all the trauma that I kept in a festering blob in the back of my head space.

How?

As a woman, this question pecked at me like birds at Tippi Hedren. How do I navigate my life when I've been programmed to conform, to withdraw, to

46

keep quiet? There was a banshee inside me waiting for the chance to scream. No organized religion provided any definitive answers. Truth be told, by my forties, I just no longer believed in a higher power of any kind other than the mysterious workings of science and nature.

Organized religion spat in the face of what I *did* believe in. Autonomy for decisions surrounding my own body, the rights of women to speak out against sexual violence, LGBTQ+ rights, transgender rights. I looked around and saw Westboro church cocksuckers filing lawsuits that the United States was being punished because of what little support homosexuals have. Cake shops refusing to cater gay weddings. Planned Parenthood under attack for giving women a choice. It kept getting worse and worse as I crept toward the 50 year old mark. Roe v. Wade was overturned. We had a numbskull fascist president who was found civilly liable for sexual assault.

More and more politicians were shouting Christian propaganda from their podiums. I began to follow an interesting little story about Arkansas Senator Jason Rapert and his crusade to erect a Ten Commandments statue on the state capitol grounds. And he did just that. He barked about how this nation is a Christian nation. So any violations of the separation of church and state is out the window, right Jason? The very foundation of our Constitutional right to Freedom of Religion means nothing. I am pretty sure we founded this country because of religious persecution, which is why we protected the right to practice our diverse religions as we see fit. Doesn't matter because … Jason said so. And he is a white man so you best fall in line.

Following directly on the ass end of his rants were the inevitable Christian anti-abortion, anti-queer, anti-trans, anti-woman horseshit arguments. If we continue to follow Rapert's lead (among so many others) and transition this secular country into a monotheistic pitchfork-wielding homo hunt, wouldn't we be changing this country into something it wasn't born as? Wouldn't we be taking a girl country and transforming it into a boy? Or vice versa? The metaphor remains. He and his kind are trying to change the baseline structure of this nation. Without its permission. Without anesthesia.

If you can do that to the country, why can't individuals do that to themselves, of their own free will? Typical hypocrisy, Jason. But hey, thanks for being so obvious about it. It helps people like me with our debates.

I was not the only one who noticed this microcosm of fuckery. Enter The Satanic Temple, a non-theological Satanic religious organization that decided to engage Jason at his own game. Founder Lucien Greaves, a kick-ass social activist with a weird eye which is the perfect look for a Satanist, petitioned the Arkansas legislature to allow the erection of a Baphomet statue. Because, after all, the Constitution protects religious freedom, and if Abrahamic religion is represented in the totally inappropriate setting of a state government capitol, then *any* religion could do the same (The ACLU also has challenged the monument's constitutionality - it ain't just the Satanists). A gorgeous Baphomet was created, sans breasts for obvious reasons, featuring the horned goat with children at the feet gazing up in admiration. The TST folks proudly unveiled it at a rally at the state capitol. Needless to say, the Christians weren't psyched about that. Baphomet was driven away after making a damn good point. I would venture to guess that if a bunch of Hindus showed up with a statue of Ganesh wanting to place it on government property, the pearls would still be clutched. Just not as tightly as with Baphomet.

Thus, the power of Satan.

Ok, I know Baphomet is not Satan but I also know these Christian morons don't see any difference. Satan scares people. Makes them wet their britches. Draws crowds of lookiloos. Gets press coverage. Writes click-bait headlines. Catch my drift?

Satan is the greatest advocate for social activism. That is what modern day Satanism is all about. Using the ultimate antagonist as an icon to shove hypocrisy into the limelight. The Ten Commandments monument battle is just a drop in the pond. TST is taking on issues like abortion rights, LGBTQ+ rights, sobriety, after school children's programs, the distribution of menstrual products to the needy, and the protection of mental health patients from pseudoscience.

It is decidedly NOT the blood-drinking sadistic Satanism I had in mind as a young teen with a copy of *The Satanic Bible* (Note: Lavey's Satanism and The Satanic Temple are very different things with very different viewpoints). Yet it is what I have landed on in my middle age. I have forgone my desires of a sexy cloven-hooved Antichrist for actual *change* in social justices and protections. These Satanists have done more to assist and speak out as allies of the disenfranchised than any other religion I know.

Recently, Louisiana passed a bill that all public classrooms must display the Ten Commandments effective November 15, 2024. Also, at the time of writing, Texas is pushing to include Bible studies in public school classrooms. So the beat goes on. Maybe by the time you are reading this, that misguided nonsense will get reversed.

Stepping on roaches won't do diddly shit until you wipe out the nest.

Ave Satanas!

Susan Snyder

Shapeshift

In middle school, I found myself in the unenviable position of having an arch nemesis. His name was Chad. He was a couple years ahead of me and took it upon himself to torture and bully me for the simple fact that I was...ugly. I suppose he was not wrong about me being ugly if I was to be compared to the societal norm. I inherited my father's nose, an impressively large one. Of course, Chad did not view my nose for the sculpture-esque wonder that it truly is. He viewed it as an affront to his hypersensitive eye holes during each and every school day.

I didn't physically develop my chesticles until high school. I was flat chested. Like, really really flat. This too was an insult to Chad and his merry band of longhairs. A preteen girl was expected to wow the crowd with womanly parts regardless of the level of maturity and hormones that were beyond her control. To be honest, I am surprised I didn't fall over frontwards from the weight of my colossal nose, so I didn't really need the additional heft of boobies to guide me into a faceplant. No one else seemed to share this appreciation for my lack of these accouterments.

Yes, Chad was a loser. But he was a popular one. He was an Adonis of golden locks and adorable boyish facial features. A bit of a metalhead. His influential hatred of me spread like rampant wildfire through the brainless masses of East Middle School. There was a target on my back.

The bus ride to and from this hellhole featured games of "keep away" using my snow hat or gloves. I was spat upon. I was on the receiving end of serenades of variations of "You ugly!" or badly rhyming renditions featuring my mother for some reason. I usually ended up in tears when I got home from school.

I sat daydreaming for hours about how I could get a nose job and breast implants at my young age. Not because I wanted any of that. I just wanted to fit in. My greatest desire was to get Chad off my fucking back.

Eventually, he went off to high school and I had a year or two of welcome reprieve. I took full advantage of this time to let my freak flag fly. I adorned myself in the fashion trends of the day such as jelly shoes, parachute pants, fluorescents, rubber bracelets, and whatever Madonna was wearing. I won countless dance contests for my high kicks and twirls at the obligatory "Night to Remember" co-ed events. I thought I was finally hot shit, boobs or no boobs. In reality, I was likely a laughing stock, since some boys would come up to me, take one look at my state of dress and ask me how much I "cost." Other girls whispered about my audacity to hit them in the face with my self-confidence as if I was an incoming pie tray filled with whipped cream.

When it was my time to attend public high school, I was ecstatic to find that Chad was not there. He was over at the local trade school. Alas, in my freshman year, I was still stuck with mosquito bites for tits and a prominent proboscis. Even without my nemesis, I still was victimized by the older popular ilk. I tried out for the cheerleading squad, which was an epic failure since I could never (still can't) get my hips to allow the splits. No one on the squad would help coach me for the tryouts, even though every other girl had their assigned mentor. At some point, I caught an older boy and his cheerleader girlfriend pointing and laughing at me. The gist seemed to be that they questioned how such an unsightly troglodyte could even be *allowed* to be in their presence. I didn't actually hear their convo, but I was most def not an idiot.

Once again, I would usually return home after school in tears.

The big change came in my sophomore year. I developed some semblance of a chest. I was thin but curvy. My face grew into my nose a bit. I made friends with some of the more influential metalhead girls in the school, which brought onto me the attention of the affiliated metalhead boys. The males might have been drawn in by my improved looks but they stuck around for how I wowed them with my encyclopedic knowledge of the lyrics of Metallica, Megadeth and the like. Truth be told, I was introduced and tutored by a male friend, who out of purely platonic altruism, made me cassette tapes of all the bands he worshiped. Not only had I found my lifelong preferred musical genre, but it gave me quite the leg up in clout with my peer group. I knew just the right time to bang my head and when to cease banging for the time change interlude, when most ignorant others would fail to cease their banging. I had a gift.

By the ripe age of fourteen, I started smoking too. At that time, that was the epitome of cool, folks. The high school even had a smoking section filled to the rim with my favorite misfits and derelicts. Seriously, those were the days.

When I was around sixteen, my mom left town and I threw a party. Word spread and I ended up with an overwhelming amount of guests, both invited and not so much. Here gathered a hodgepodge of characters ranging from my bestie girlfriend to my makeshift personal bodyguard, Glen, an older gentle giant of a man who had served time for manslaughter (the victim guy deserved it) and was very protective of me. Most importantly, guess who showed up at my little soiree?

Chad.

Years had passed since Chad had a gander at his younger tormentee. He had no idea who I was, but I recognized him immediately. By this time, I was popular enough for word about my party to infiltrate the deep recesses of Chad's orbit of trade school social circles. He looked the same. I did not.

I played it pretty cool for the first hour or so. He made a beeline for me and my now appealing visage. He hovered around me like an irritating hornet. I went out to have a ciggie, he went out to have a ciggie. I went to grab a beer, he went to grab a beer. He would be there waiting outside the bathroom door when I went to take a piss. My annoyance threshold reached critical mass and I couldn't wait any longer for the big reveal.

Rustling through a desk drawer, I found my instrument of revenge. My East Middle School yearbook, circa 6th grade. Opening to the page featuring my ugly duckling school photo, I slammed it down on my dining room table. My blackened long index fingernail pointed to the little girl that offended Chad's discerning ways for so long.

Confused, he asked, "Who's that?" Christ, he didn't even remember his target of unhinged sadism.

"That's me."

Chuckling. "That's not you!"

"It is me."

A crowd gathered around. Some backed me up that it was indeed a picture of me. Some commented on the astounding difference from then to now. I watched the color drain out of Chad's already pale face.

"Wow!" he exclaimed. "You have definitely changed for the better!" More chuckling but now, it seemed a little trepidatious.

Now for the coup de grace.

"Glen?" Glen's the big scary sweet manslaughter dude I told you about. He was about 6'4", 250 pounds, dark and bearded, tattooed and pierced through every place you could thread a needle. He needed no prompting as he walked toward Chad, forcing Chad to walk backwards toward the back door, hands up in a "have mercy" plea.

Chad was well aware of who I was at that point.

Glen got him to the threshold of the duplex's back porch, spun him around and grabbed the back of Chad's jeans and the neck of his concert tee, gripping onto some of his golden locks in the process. Heave ho and out he went. He flew about fifteen feet through the air and landed face down on the front lawn. Once he regained his bearings, he fled on foot, scurrying like a rat from rising floodwater.

The friends he arrived with did not follow. Instead they erupted in howls of laughter. There was applause. Everyone understood what happened even if they weren't witnesses to my degradation in middle school. It gave all my party guests something to talk about as they drank their cans of Natty Lights.

I jumped into Glen's arms, wrapping my legs and arms around him and pecking him incessantly on his giant fuzzy cheek. He spun me around with glee. I mean, he really dug the opportunity to intimidate people. I loved him so much for that.

During that time and for long after, I was a sexual firestorm. I viewed my sex appeal as a weapon of control to be wielded, a magical superpower. As I explained earlier, this was all my contrived deranged replacement for my father's love. But there were too many villains stepping up to challenge my female prowess. I got defeated... a lot. Traumatically.

When I should have been the most vivacious and self-confident in my life, I always felt like I was held captive by someone like Chad, bound and dangling above a pool with sharks with lasers on their heads. Sometimes I was dropped in to be torn apart quickly. Sometimes I just spun excruciatingly slowly toward my demise. My femininity was just a piece of meat hung on a hook to be devoured.

The thing about sharks, lasers or not, is that the males have two dicks. You may not have been aware of that. I say this to point out that, although the threat may already be bad, it can be worse than you thought. Double worse.

Susan Snyder

Slut

I didn't have my first orgasm until I was around 28 years old. I know most folk would say, "You just hadn't found the right man!" But I'd had a lot of sex by then with dozens of men. I just found the whole thing quite boring. I didn't have sex because I enjoyed it per se. It was my desperate attempt to replace my father's love by pleasing men. Not myself. Men.

Regardless of my misplaced intentions, I still got the lovely reputation of being a slut. If they meant "slut" as a term for a promiscuous woman, then I suppose they were correct. But why does it have such a bad connotation? I mean, there I was, spreading joy across the land to any dude who looked at me. Shouldn't I get a fucking medal or something? I wasn't spreading STDs or humping married men. Men got pleasure out of it. I was a vaginal hero. Sheena, Queen of the Slut People.

I, on the other hand, did not in return receive

pleasure.

I was just going through the motions. Taking it like a sexual automaton. Even when I didn't want to have sex, I was easy convinced otherwise, as the guy proceeded to fuck me anyway. Look, I am not saying I was raped. Well, I was but that's for the next chapter. These instances were more of a gray area. If you don't say "no" and you don't put up a physical resistance, how is the guy to know? I'll be honest in saying my coital suitors were not the brightest bulbs in the pack. And this was the late eighties and into the nineties. Rape was still a taboo subject in which women took most of the blame. We didn't know we could speak out publicly and point a finger yet.

Consent is super cut and dry when you're discussing an unconscious, threatened, incapacitated, or verbally rejective person. My incapacity was not with zip ties or at gunpoint (well, that happened, but again…next chapter). In these gray cases, my insides, my psyche said "no." That was not verbally expressed to the man. I suppose the tightening of my muscles, the clenched jaw, the furrowed brow might have indicated that I wasn't into it. I was just holding my breath and letting it happen. That's what I thought I was expected to do, supposed to do. Should a man pick up on these subtle signals and interpret them as non-consent? Perhaps. I would like to hope that any grown man would. Would a sixteen, eighteen, twenty year old?

I can't answer that but, truthfully, I just don't know if they had the experience or upbringing to know better.

If you're thinking that I am walking the razor's edge of defending men who continue their sexual conquests despite the woman clearly grinning and bearing it, I'm gonna stop you right there. I am certainly not. All men should know better. They should be *taught* to know better from an early age. Check in with the partner. Ask for consent. All that. My point is to just say that *in my personal case* I was not very clear about any of it. And *in my personal case*, specifically these gray area encounters, I take some responsibility in that moment. Now, how I got to that moment might be a whole other discussion and there may be some shifting of responsibility within that. I'm not letting guys off the hook, sisters. Unclench the pearls.

Speaking of the era of this time, I was part of the metal scene. Good metal and bad metal. I used a can of AquaNet a week to keep my hair high and my self-esteem low. My short skirt and chunky heels made me stand out like a platinum blonde billboard Barbie. This was what us female fans of glam metal would do, y'all. It was the uniform. Not all metalhead men would notice jeans and concert tees. I just had to dress for my audience. That's how you put butts in the seats, kids.

With this scantily clad wardrobe, attention was indeed gotten. I sexualized myself. Again, I wasn't exactly privy to the fact that I could walk down a street stark ass naked and men still don't have the right to fuck me without my say so. Because of my flagrant disregard for my own self-worth, and my desire for any guy's affection, I walked right into the lion's den. I take some responsibility here. Me. I am only talking about myself here. I speak for no one else.

Not every encounter was tedium. I chased some of them down like a slasher killer let loose in the swimsuit portion of a beauty pageant. When I netted my prize, however, I was always just disappointed. Same ol' same sex. Boring Lots of thrusting. I never let a guy go down on me. I recall thinking that was a bit much. Too intimate. Too gross. An intense paranoia would overcome me if a male's face started heading to the land down under. What if I had a yeast infection? Odor? Bits of toilet paper stuck in lickable places? In retrospect, that is the chance they were taking in this choice, and also, I was shockingly unaware of the power of my own clitoris at this time. So, back to just thrusting and lassitude.

You're welcome for the sex act, man person. Do you love me now? No? Alrighty then.

NEXT!

Relationships were a joke to me. Those superficial ones that I developed, faded quickly as I simply got disenchanted with the whole ordeal. No semblance of love was ever enough. I wanted more. I wanted all of them. I wanted fatherly love. And ain't no man going to be able to fill those shoes. Romantic relationships were barking up the wrong species of the affection tree, I am aware. If those got fatherly, then there is something assuredly wrong and someone needs to call the police. Yet, I had no clue I was such a broken shell, running about town trying to get her holes filled.

I totally mixed up my holes. Whoopsie. My bad!

Flash forward to when I was 28-ish and that first orgasm I spoke of. I knew of this phenomenon known as an "orgasm" but it seemed like a copulation cryptid to me. No sighting or evidence. Just anecdotal talk from other women. Someone told me it was a sensation not unlike needing to pee really bad. That sounded unpleasant. Shit, I pee a little when I sneeze, so how is that feeling any big whoop? Later, I would come to realize that description was a bit off.

I never learned how to ride a bike. Ever. No one ever taught me and I wasn't particularly interested. I couldn't let this orgasm thing be like that. I had to figure this shit out.

One afternoon, I went to my room and played with myself to see if I could summon this carnal knowledge. It took a while, I ain't gonna lie. I knew, instinctively, I needed to focus on the little man in the boat. Finally, I did find myself thinking I needed to take an urgent piss. Yet, it was not that. I kept going. It got more and more intense until I finally achieved the holy grail of whoopee. My mom was in the other room (yes, I lived with my mom at the age of 28 and who are you to judge?). I had to keep my vocal utterings to a minimum, which was hard considering this was my very first orgasm. The first one is quite the epiphany, I gotta admit.

After, I just lay there contemplating what the fuck just happened and how I missed this for so long. Or maybe how *they* missed this for so long. I thought back to all those times I refused cunnilingus. At that moment, I knew what I must do.

Soon after, I began dating a very buff man with GQ cover looks. Hubba hubba. All we really did was fuck so I'm not sure if "dating" is the right word. The guy was a dim-witted gym freak that only conversed about his biceps. At any rate, during one of our hookups, he started traveling downtown. Ah, but this time, I allowed it! Lo and behold, I had my first orgasm during an actual sexual encounter with someone else.

Henceforth, oral sex became a demand, nay, a command to any partner who wanted to get with me. He had to ring the doorbell to come inside. Sex transformed into less of a despairing and bastardized form of therapy to an enjoyable endeavor.

Ironically, my reproductive organs turned my life into an obstacle course of pain, fibroids, cysts, and malaise just as I figured all this out. A slut of my stature, having unlocked the key to her coronation into the echelon of sex babes, got knocked off the throne. I had less sex from then on than when I was a benumbed strumpet. There have been times (like at the time of writing this) that I've gone months, even a year, without fornicating. The pain wouldn't let me.

I chalk this up to the elementary school dick-kicking karma. Let this be a word to the wise. No matter how young or naive you might be, don't kick innocent little dicks. Save that for the ones who deserve it. As all the ladies know, we will inevitably meet a man who deserves it at some point.

Susan Snyder

Shame

The man seemed nice enough. My friendly nature toward strangers led to a cordial discussion with this guy, who sat alone on the stone wall along Wollaston Beach. Just small talk, really. On this day, even though I was seventeen and still in the thralls of my glam metal phase, I was dressed casually in shorts and a baggy tee shirt. My friends were already fading into the distance as I walked toward where my mom's car was parked. She let me use it from time to time since I had fairly recently acquired my driver's license. It was twilight and the sun was slipping slowly away.

I mumbled some version of goodbye to this amicable stranger. He asked for a hug. I look back and know full damn well that allowing this hug was my critical mistake. Now, half way through the 2020's, no stranger, no matter how polite they seem, would get a fucking hug. Back then, I just thought if I was nice, they would be too. I trusted people. I wasn't in a back bedroom at a headbanger party. I wasn't in a back alley. I was at a public beach that still had a semblance of sunlight illuminating the granite in the stones and glinting off car hoods. There were not a lot of folks milling around since it was early fall, and although it was unseasonably warm that day, families and working folks had better things to do than hang out at a grimy and practically unswimmable stretch of coastline. The horseshoe crabs hadn't begun their mating invasion yet, taking up most of the sandy real estate, which always brought lookiloos who would molest the poor things as they tried to produce their progeny.

As I hugged this guy as gingerly as I could muster, trying to keep a safe distance between any of my woman parts and him, I felt the cold metal through my tee shirt. He whispered to me not to scream and to come with him.

I didn't know if the gun was loaded and I didn't care to find out. He opened the back door of his nearby sedan and pushed me inside. He closed the door behind him. I twisted my body around in the confined space of the back bench seat so I didn't keep my back to him. As I did this in the span of about five seconds, seventeen years worth of thoughts circled my brain. As they swirled, the rest of me was lacking any feeling whatsoever. I knew I was going to be raped. Any idea of trying to get myself the fuck out of this did not make any appearance inside my tornado of thoughts.

I was resigned to this happening. I just lay there for a while as he fumbled with my shorts and underwear, my upper shoulders, neck and head awkwardly pressed up against the roll-down window handle on the back door. He struggled to put on a condom with his free hand and he held the gun to my midriff with the other. I recall being thankful for the condom. I couldn't call the escape thoughts up to bat, but gratitude for a rubber was what stepped to the podium? Bizarre, right?

After he penetrated me for a minute or two, he seemed aggravated at the lack of wiggle room and grabbed me under my armpits to arrange me on his lap in one swift and precise motion. He kept my shirt and bra on. Maybe that would be too obvious to any walkers-by that saw me topless sitting on a dude in the back of a car. The gun pointed at my face, he maneuvered my hips by using his other hand to guide me into what he wanted me to do. I had no fucking clue what to do, gun or no gun. I wasn't a virgin but I sure as hell was a back seat rape virgin.

Numbness. Embarrassment. Disbelief. I don't remember too much other than that. What I do remember was the smell of The Clam Box restaurant close by, across the street from this strip of parking spaces along the beachfront. The greasy, fishy smell of fried clams and plump hot dogs. There is some morbose humor in that, isn't there? A macabre analogy. At some point, I wondered if the smell was coming from between my legs or from the restaurant. Or if one was overtaking the other. My mind went to some surly places when finding myself in the midst of a sexual assault that began as a hug.

To be honest, I never thought he was going to kill me. Or if I did, I didn't seem to care, in retrospect. I wanted this over with. I wanted to get back into my mom's car and drive home. I wanted to take a shower. I wanted to go to bed.

And I eventually did just that.

One thing I never did is tell anyone about this. Stay calm and act natural. Go about your business. Nothing to see here.

At first, in the day or two following the incident, I blamed myself for being too friendly, too trusting. I had it coming by giving some stranger the time of day. And I *hugged him!* I asked for it. I didn't put up a fight or cry out for help. I didn't drive to the nearest police station and barge in to report the dastardly deed.

I was embarrassed. Mortified. Wasn't there a distinct and personally obvious difference between this act of sex, forced at gunpoint, and the couple (to this point) of young guys, my age, who had taken advantage of my ineptitude at expressing my non-consent? But was there really a difference? I went limp as overcooked spaghetti either way. I resolved myself to just shut up and take it. That's what the menfolk wanted at those moments, and clearly, a gun didn't make much of an impact on how I reacted to that.

Hey look, the statute of limitations has long since run out on doing anything about what happened that day. After time went by, I chalked it up to how things were for a female. No one spoke about this shit. Women fumbled through life side-stepping and swerving away from dicks and hands like a game of dodgeball. We had to learn how to be hypervigilant, scanning our surroundings with, what we hoped would be, accuracy. Kind of failed that in my case, don't ya think?

Not every devil appears in his true form, however. A sparkling spectrum of sociopaths and narcissists are always there somewhere. Like pollen wafting from trees, you might not see it at all until you get into the right light. Oh yes, there are signs of their presence. The pollen makes you sneeze and your eyes water. You become fatigued trying to fight off the symptoms. Once in a while, you'll fall victim to a full blown attack, knocking you down for a while. Periods of time will be quiet, as the spores and specks settle back into the soil, back into the cycle from whence they came.

But if you're a woman, you know they'll return. You begin again the exhausting toil of rebuilding your tolerance for enduring them and failing to comprehend your shocking lack of immunity against them. We have no pill to pop to assist us. No antihista-"men."

Alas, from the grope in a holiday shopping crowd to a date rape to a gang rape to a much much worse situation, we women have to fear it. From the spiritual guru to the family member to the boyfriend to the man featured on the latest episode of "Very Scary People," we women have to expect it and guard ourselves against it. What makes us a woman gets turned into a seminal receptacle or an internal boxing ring for a power struggle.

Am I exaggerating? Do you honestly think so? I, personally, have NEVER met a woman who hasn't had something done to her which violates her in a sexual manner. And hey, we *talk* about these things now. We make documentaries and podcasts about them. We share on social media despite the trolls and the threatening comments. We even have to be hypervigilant about even *talking about* this shit lest we be blindsided by the vitriolic ejaculations of those who don't believe women should gather any strength, especially in numbers.

I am very outspoken about the rights of females now that I'm in my middle age. Still, this was the first time I've exposed what happened to me on that particular day at Wollaston Beach. Everyone knows that sexual violence is under reported. Why is that? Perhaps, like me, some women are just anesthetized to the trauma. To this day, I don't feel any type of way about that rape at gunpoint. I mean, I'm fairly sure I do deep deep down in my trenches, but maybe not. I didn't feel any type of way in the moment of being raped. I felt like I set that wheel in motion by my innocent hug. The assault wasn't anything truly unexpected. I was raised in a time where that was part of being a woman. We just rolled with it. What would happen if I spoke out about it? Nada. Nothing. So what was the point in trying? To be looked at as damaged goods wasn't what I was all about. I wanted to come off as strong and fearless. I had other shit to do besides sit around and feel bad about it. Had to keep growing up. Had to get through school. Had to keep up the strength to dodge and weave dicks and hands like a good woman should.

I am fifty fucking years old and now, just *now*, I am able to speak up and speak out. I honestly am unsure if it will make any difference today, just as I doubted it would back then. Yet, I won't give up trying. What else can I do?

The numbness that overtook me like a venereal disease is likely just the top layer of the onion. Somewhere, in layer 245, there is a ticking time bomb of traumatic response patiently awaiting its time in the spotlight. A dormant big bang of screaming and weeping and panting to catch my breath between sobs of outrage and in-rage. Will I ever reach that layer? You'd think with all the true crime shows and depraved extreme horror novels, I would have been triggered by now.

The only way I, as a woman, can survive is to keep the onion from peeling too far down. True, even the outer layers of an onion can make me cry. Despite the years of insensate acceptance of things being just as they are and always have been. Should I continue to chalk up my tears as a dismissable reaction to a fetid and malodorous situation? Or should I delve down deeper and explore what lies beneath, no matter the deluge of emotions that might release?

Hey, I wrote this book. I have been brutally honest with you, my dear reader. Maybe that's enough for now. Maybe each page is another layer laid bare. A peeling that brings me one step closer to healing. A healing peeling.

I am not quite ready to write page 245 just yet. Probably never will be. Can you convince me that there is some stage of womanhood when I will be safe? A time when I can finally let my guard down? When I don't have to be in a state of permanent caution? If you know, please tell me.

Until then, I'll stay in survival mode. As is a woman's custom.

Persecution

A picture of an ex-boyfriend popped up on social media today. I almost threw up my Honey Nut Cheerios. It's not nice to say you hate someone, that you wouldn't bat an eye if you heard he died horrifically in an acid bath. Yet, here we are.

I'll be nice enough to change his name to, shall we say, G. G was not the only toxic and abusive man I have had the pleasure of relating with. I would have to write a tome the size of *War and Peace* to regale you with all my stories of ghastly partners. So for now, let's focus on some highlights.

But let's back up a bit first. I want to discuss what led up to this particular love disaster. It has been extremely hard for me to find a man who treats me nicely, respectfully. If you are a nice man, super! I am not talking about you. If you are someone who is in a relationship with a nice man, goodie gumdrops! I am speaking about me and my experiences. So step into my icicle-ridden den of persecution and take my bony hand in yours as we trip the light fantastic all over my pain.

I was a mall rat in my early teens. Here, I met my first semblance of a boyfriend at the ripe age of thirteen. His name was L and he was very sweet. We didn't kiss or anything. We hung out in front of the Record Town in the South Shore Plaza. Still reeling from the lack of an active father, I was chuffed as punch to get the attention of any man child. L was mostly harmless. The only mistake he made was giving me my very first taste of liquor. A bunch of us rats shared a bottle of Peppermint Schnapps on the top of the parking garage. I might have had the equivalent of one shot but I think I puked up the part of my brain that had any common sense. Did some permanent damage to it anyway.

One night he tried to convince me to take a ride with his fourteen year old ass in a stolen vehicle. I hesitated and eventually declined. He proceeded to wrap it around a telephone pole and send himself to the hospital, where he spent time in a coma and woke to a severe and debilitating brain injury. I felt horrible for him but also thanked my lucky stars I didn't join him in his joyride. He communicated with me only through typing. He couldn't walk or speak. His mind was stuck in the pre-wreck moment. For years, he thought we were still a couple. I had long since moved on and lost interest in writing letters back or visiting him in the rehab. Teenage girls are little selfish twats. I was no different.

The first major relationship came when I was fifteen, and the related story of losing my virginity is told in another chapter. This guy, R, was the keyboard player for a Bon Jovi wannabe hair band. Filled to the rim with narcissism and self-importance, he truly believed that I had to rearrange myself to uphold his image. He dictated the way I dressed and how I did my hair. He often bamboozled my mom into driving me to his family home, leaving me there for an hour, and picking me back up. Like it was an innocent time we were spending together. What the fuck do you think this nineteen year old dude was doing with your fourteen year old daughter for an hour? The best part is that he would steal my underwear and hang it on his wall among all the other girls' panties that he took as post-coital trophies. One time, I was expecting my period so I had a panty liner just in case I started bleeding. He snatched my undies and was horrified to discover this baffling object. He had no fucking clue what a panty liner was or what it might be for. Clearly, it meant something, and that something must be vagina-related and nefarious.

Fast forward to the next time I went to see his band rehearse in the studio. He had told the band all about this and I was derided for this perceived abominable panty liner until I ran out of there crying. He also gave me chlamydia and told the band and their hangers-on that I gave it to him. I was the glam metal Hester Prynne after that. Blindsided and ashamed, I was so inexperienced that I believed I actually gave it to him. In reality, he was the first and *only* man I had ever been with. It was impossible for me to contract an STD unless that prick gave it to *me*. Which, of course he did. Turns out he bareback tapped a hooker at a Motley Crue concert while we were dating.

Another time, this animal brought me to a party and held me down on my belly so his bandmates could take turns fondling my butt. Granted, my butt was nothing short of spectacular, but I didn't give anyone the greenlight for a mass molestation. Directly following this, he took me into someone's Camaro and finger-fucked me until I bled.

Oh the memories.

When I eventually moved away from this bullshit, I stayed within my comfortable orbit of guys who used more Aqua Net than I did and considered themselves "musicians." Enter the tight-jeaned, big-haired loser we'll refer to as J. Since I was anguished and clinging to any male attention, I ignored J's tendency to simply use me for the fact that I actually had a place to live. He wooed me into thinking I loved him (I was fifteen) and under threat of him moving away to Florida and leaving me forever, I convinced my mom to let him move in with us. To this day, I am shocked that she let this happen. She even let him sleep with me in my room. Again, what did you think we were doing in there, Ma? Playing Yahtzee?

For a while, it was fine. We all got along and enjoyed some genuine gut-busting laughter. Then one fine day, J didn't like the cut of my jib and slammed me into the radiator, nearly breaking my ribs and causing quite the impressive bruise around my torso. There was hairpulling at times and lots of demeaning insults. I told my mom about this. She didn't believe me. This guy charmed my own mother onto his side. With no savior in sight, the abuse continued unchecked. Finally, J made the mistake of pushing me down and kicking at my stomach… in front of my mother. This took away her blindfold and my mom freaked out. I can't remember if we called the cops or what the fuck we did, but he skeedaddled.

A few days later, I got home from school to find two older girls who looked like they walked off the set of a Britny Fox video. They were waiting in my front yard and proceeded to attack me. One grabbed my arms from the back while the other stood in front of me spewing insults. She might as well have had "J told me to say this" blinking overhead in neon lights. Always the scrapper, I scraped my Doc Marten down the shin of the girl behind me and stomped her foot with all my might. That loosened her grip and my arms were suddenly free. I wound my right one back and gave an uppercut to the girl in front of me. This was not part of the hit job, so they fled in an El Camino.

If he couldn't get me, he'd send his pussy posse over to get me. After that epic fail, he never bothered me again.

Skipping ahead to my thirties, everything between J and G were more covers of the same tired song. I drank a little socially. My career was focused on teaching yoga and working at yoga studios. My core muscles were on point. I thought I had matured, grown wise and found a path to a thread of the tapestry of enlightenment.

G was allegedly a yogi too. He volunteered at a yoga studio I worked at and, thinking he was a like minded truth-seeker, I became smitten. He had a kid, which normally was a deal breaker for me. But his daughter, it would turn out, was the only good thing I encountered in this debacle. I was still a social drinker but he took drinking to a whole different level. It wasn't the volume as much as the inconsistency around it. We would drink beer every night for a bit then, when I would show up to his place with the usual expected supply, he would switch gears and make me out to be an alcoholic force feeding him this elixir in direct opposition to our lives as proper yogis.

I had a pit bull at the time, a rescue as a puppy who had a lot of behavioral issues. He was very protective of me and could be a little skittish to men who came around. I adored that dog. One day, G and his daughter, who he had custody of on the weekends, were out on the porch with the dog. G insisted that my dog tried to attack his daughter. Now, whether or not that is true is up in the air since I wasn't present. Nevertheless, G did not shut up about how dangerous my dog was and how it needed to be put down for the safety of all mankind. When I brought up the fact that this was *my kid* he was talking about, he lost it. He got in my face and ranted poetically about how I was a worthless whore of a woman who would never comprehend what it's like to actually have a *kid*. He pushed me out his door and told me to "fuck off." He said that a lot to me after that. "Fuck off." I sat in my car in his apartment complex, shell-shocked that this guy, who I thought walked on water, would turn on a dime like that. He apologized later, but the stance on mandatory euthanasia for my dog never let up.

I know what you're thinking. I told him "fuck off" right back and left him in my dust. Nope. I was already so broken by then and so desperate for my one, my savior, someone who loved me, that I allowed myself to be brainwashed into putting my dog down. My friends came over and comforted me but I could tell that they were dumbstruck that I actually did that. I have never forgiven myself. I will never forgive myself. My shame overrides any recognition that I was emotionally abused into it. I mean, I know that the psychological damage he was inflicting on me led to it. *I know.* But how can you ever get right with yourself after unnecessarily having your vet kill an innocent dog? Every dog since has been pampered and put high on a pedestal. Yet, I'll never ever shake what happened to that one.

And I will never shake the hatred I have for G for making me do it.

I still didn't walk away. When I told him that my dog had been put down, he told me that I was crazy if I thought he cared at all. I was a useless bitch and no dead dog would change that. G gave zero fucks about the emotional damage he was causing me. It was about to get worse.

We moved in together (I know, I know) and eventually his best friend came to live with us to cut down the expenses. We drank like fishes. We got another dog together (I KNOW!). Every day was a battle for my soul. I wanted to get out of there but the lease was under my name. The idea of kicking G out seemed impossible. I just didn't have the brass balls to pull it off. I had constant bladder infections, bacterial infections, panic attacks. I thought I was going to die on the daily. Sometimes he would corner me for hours and just yell hurtful insults in my face. Once it was because I loaded the dishwasher improperly. Another time, he stabbed me with a fork because he wanted the last of the delicious whatever that was on my plate. *My* plate. That I cooked and paid for. Then he scolded me for scolding him.

Then there was the sex stuff.

Most relationships, in the beginning, are happy times when you fuck like rabbits. And it was. As the emotional abuse ramped up, I became scared of G. I truly thought I loved him but I sure as hell didn't like him anymore. Most of my energy was presenting as daydreaming about how I could get myself out of it. Most of *his* energy was spent guilting me into sex and making me experience terror every night, when I just wanted to get some sleep. I'm not claiming he raped me. It's more complex than that. It was a breakdown of who I was as a woman, my role in the relationship, over years of time. Almost every night, I would await the onslaught of him initiating sex. The only reprieves were when I had my period (although that didn't always stop him) or when we were fighting. My refusal to participate, no matter the biological or defensive reason for the refusal, was the main trigger point in a ton of arguments.

The fact of the matter is that I was beginning to really hate the guy. Constantly barraged with insults, my mental health was disintegrating. My drinking amped up into an epic self-prescribed medication to escape from my reality. I was a full fledged functioning alcoholic. I probably drank, on average, about a six-pack per night. G was always a participant but made sure never to admit that. It was all me. I was the drunk, the skank, the prude, the hypocrite. I was the bane of his existence. I would drink every night until I would miss or show up late to work regularly because I was nursing a hangover. I needed someone to help me. I needed a safe space to heal and recover. I needed love.

True to form, G picked the time when I was at my lowest to break up with me, when he was dropping me off at the bus station as I headed to work. When I begged him to, rather than abandon me, help me get off the sauce and heal our relationship, he reeled back his fist and barked at me to get the fuck out of his car. Not the first time he expressed keen interest in wanting to punch me. In fact, his bestie was the one who told me that he had been married before he met me. He also told me that he was arrested for beating his ex-wife to within an inch of her life. G failed to mention that to me. Oh and he kicked the shit out of the girl he dated right before me. This led to him having to do a bunch of community service and spending a weekend in jail. She had a restraining order against him when we started dating. I knew he had to do community service, but again, he failed to mention the full story of *why*.

I guess I was lucky that he held back his maniacal ways to just verbal and emotional abuse. I'm not sure why he never hit me. Maybe he knew if he did it again, he would be slammed with a felony and spend some quality time in the hoosegow. After all, with me, he figured out how to do maximum damage to his partner without the hassle of having to bruise his pretty knuckles. Clever.

We were still in the ill-advised process of reconciliation (ok, ok, I know! Hang on!) when I went on a weekend women's yoga retreat on the Gulf Coast. I texted him on the way there with a jolly "Have a good weekend." His response was a tirade on how much of a bitch I was for even saying that, knowing he had to work all weekend and blah, blah, blah. Something in my brain pan snapped. At long last, after many years of dealing with this cunt of a man, I got it. I understood what he was doing. What he had done. He didn't give two flying fucks about me. Never had. He was a sociopathic narcissist.

I ghosted him. Blocked him on everything. Never communicated with him again.

That, my friends, was the best thing I'd ever done in my entire life. Now, a decade after that last text, his stupid face popped up on my social media. To be honest, I was bummed out that he was still alive.

There is a movement around the world currently where men are forming a giant circle jerk of superiority over women. This anti-feminist, pro-bro-dude bubble is just a more public and organized expression of more of the same. In Kenya, it's called the "Manosphere." We have the "Your body, my choice" slogan right here at home. Ain't that a hoot? Men like Andrew Tate and Donald Trump are feeding this beast and social media spews it into our face like patriarchal bukkake. My question is why are these men, like the ones I've dated, so threatened by women? What have we done to make you hate us so much? What have we done to make you make us hate *ourselves* so much?

I look back on all my relationship struggles now and scratch my head. I would never say that I have been a perfect embodiment of all things altruistic and benevolent. I have always been, and remain, a mess. Still, I wonder what I did that was so diabolical that I deserved to go through this abuse at the hands of men. Multiple men. Like I said, these are just a few highlights from the extensive reel of my life's crappy romantic life. What did I do to them?

Was it karma from the elementary school dick-kicking? Probably not, but I would be lying if I said that didn't cross my mind. In reality, the penis punishment of my youth was most likely a preemptive strike against my future abuse. A foreshadowing defense impulse.

For any man who chooses to join the ranks of incels and misogynists, I want to extend my most whole-hearted wishes for you to "fuck off." Really, I mean that from the bottom of my scarified and pummeled heart. From what G taught me, it seems like a sentiment you might truly understand.

Oh by the way:

Panty Liner = "...to absorb everyday vaginal discharge, unexpected light period flow, light spotting, staining at the beginning and ends of

periods, and post-intercourse discharge..."
The more you know.

Susan Snyder

Covens

Truth-seeking women, who are already transformed by life into dried out sponges eager to suck up any moisture with the potential to heal, are prime candidates to be recruited into a cult. I, for one, joined three of them.

Cults are not inherently obvious to spot. They are insidious. They sneak up on you. Not unlike abusive people, they start off harmless and wait for you to let your guard down before they morph into psychic vampires who like to use their power in villainous ways. It's easy for us to point and laugh at how idiotic anyone is who allows themselves to fall prey to these covens of madness. Cults grow in numbers for a reason, folks. I would argue that if you are one of the approximately 1.3 billion members of the Catholic Church, you are in a cult. Hey, a lot of the same warning signs are hiding under every pew and chasuble. Churches wield spiritual authority while they secretly fondle kids and ask you for money. It's a fucking cult.

While I was working and teaching for a yoga studio, they were gracious enough to allow me to take teacher training for free. One of these was training in Kundalini yoga, a fairly niche yoga lineage that was growing in popularity in the 2010s. Have you ever seen a bunch of yoga students walking into a studio wearing all white, sporting white turbans and smelling of patchouli and/or body odor? Yah, that's them.

Well, I should say, that was *us*.

I felt pressured to learn about this technology by my dearest mentor at the time, a devotee to Kundalini and Vedic Astrology. In no way am I blaming him for my introduction to this. He is a victim of a very manipulative, charismatic and attractive leader, just like the rest of us. The fault of the pain this cult caused lies solely on Yogi Bhajan, a man who bastardized the religion of Sikhism and took hold of the hippie counterculture in the West. Among the reimagined versions of ancient yoga practices like Ashtanga, Anusara, Iyengar, Viniyoga and many others, this one stands alone. It is its own animal. Kundalini is not beneficial to your physical body at all, and in fact, it can really wreck your physical body. The goal here is to jack up your nervous system into a state of being high. Very fucking high. There are reasons and excuses for everything from the head wraps to the white to abstaining from alcohol, drugs, sex and meat. Rather than mantras in Sanskrit, you chant or sing in Gurmukhi, a Sikh based Indian language. Greetings are blurted out as "Sat Nam" instead of "Namaste." I even got a spiritual name from the 3HO organization... Sham Sundar Kaur. That means twilight, or the color of Krishna's skin. Whatever.

At one of the mandatory weekend retreats during training, I spoke my objections to the entire practice to my mentor. I told him this was a cult and dangerous to most who were in attendance. My mentor wasn't offended since he was already quite accustomed to my anti-establishment rantings. He just asked me to give it a chance. Fair enough. We also had to attend a White Tantric session where Kundalinis gather en masse to endure ridiculous sets of kriyas and meditations. I lucked out, since that year, we only had to hold off on blinking, keep our arms raised overhead or contort our spines for eleven to thirty-ish minutes at a time. Often, these exercises in torture could last sixty-ish minutes to several hours. Have you ever held your arms overhead for an hour? It fucking sucks. The eye-watering pain changes into a complete disassociation with the fact that you even have arms. Who knows what that is supposed to help with. Balancing your chakras? Elevating your energy? Annihilating your shoulder sockets? Your guess is as good as mine.

I also lucked out on the fact that Yogi Bhajan had already croaked by this time. Over the years since, the exposure of his abuse towards his disciples, mostly toward women and children, has been coming in fast and hot. It is now widely known that his close harem of women, who he referred to as "secretaries," were brainwashed into serving his every whim. He forced them to provide sexual favors, groom other women, or even flat out raped them. Oh, and rape isn't really a thing, you see. Here is a lovely quote direct from the mouth of this shining light of spiritual guidance:

"Rape is always invited. It never happens. A person who is raped is always providing subconsciously the environments and the arrangements. If you do not provide the circumstances and the arrangements, it is impossible."

Brilliant way to sweep your predatory behavior under the rug, douchebag. Imagine how the violated women must have felt when they were the ones to blame according to their guru. Fancy how easy it would be for the other men inside this twisted organization to enact his ways into their own lives. After all, it can't happen unless we women set it all up to happen.

Suffice to say, I didn't spend much time within this woo woo cult after I received my certification. My boyfriend, G, did. When it comes to yogic fruit of a poisoned tree, G was licking the sap from its trunk. Being a sex-obsessed narcissistic sociopathic hypocrite, he fit right in.

A few years later, I unsuspectingly joined another cult. Well, this one might have been a little more obvious, but my teacher's sexual appetite didn't rear its ugly head until later. I met this teacher through the same yoga studio that thrust me into Kundalini. He was young, charming, tattooed and good looking and was not only a Sanskrit and Vedic scholar, but a practitioner of Chinese medicine. I began to see him for astrology readings and acupuncture. Here's a bit of wisdom for you: do not let anyone do a private astrology reading who has any inkling of suspicious intentions. Through the reading and bombardment of personal questions, you are going to reveal a lot, too much, information to this person. If you offer up a weakness or vulnerability, buckle up for that to be wielded over you like the Sword of Damocles.

So this mentor of mine took me under his wing, but in such a strange way. He not only introduced me to the wacky world of left-hand Tantric practices (black sex magic of a sort) but also to his own mentor, who was even more full of himself. At one point I did a Gnostic eucharist, which caused an unexpected flashback to my Catholic upbringing. This version was much more embracing of secret teachings and occult arts. I mean, I dug it but I also felt that if I was wrong about the falsehood of the church, I would surely be struck down by the hand of God by doing these darker rituals. I don't believe

I was wrong about the church, yet that Catholic guilt persists.

My teacher, call him C, would email me and call me often to spout gossip about who, in the yoga community, he would like to fuck and who was a total cunt. He sent me a video of him filming an amateur porn on the very table where I got my acupuncture treatments. He sent me a dick pic. Does this seem like something a spiritual mentor and trusted medical authority should be doing? Well, you get the gold star. I, on the other hand, fell into it hook, line and sinker. He made it seem that I was the *only one* he could trust to share his deepest inner thoughts and impressively sized appendages. Me being singled out as his confidant took perfect advantage of my susceptibility toward attention. Especially *male* attention.

As I moved deeper into the trough of Kool-Aid, I came to learn from women that I, myself, had personally gotten involved in this; that C had been doing some bad shit. One woman had him almost break up her marriage. Another was sexually abused when he convinced her it would help her spiritual growth and womanly issues if he examined her. It turned into a non-consensual sexual act that scarred this wonderful woman. C was good, really good at manipulating people. He made it quite clear to me that it was a goal of his to do so. Once I heard these stories, I was out. Everything became crystal clear. I vomited the

Kool-Aid in the nearest trash bin and ran for the fucking hills.

I didn't just run. I called his employer and reported that they were working with a sexual predator. No response. I contacted a few of his own teachers who had endorsed his writings and teachings in the past. The response was exactly on par with how an ostrich buries its head in the sand. Didn't want to get involved. Outta sight, outta mind. I tried to offer my support to the women who I introduced to him, and tried to apologize for my lack of insight into this crap. No one told me it was my fault, but holy hell, do I have lingering bad thoughts about my role in it all.

He had successfully pulled his charismatic wool over my gullible eyes.

Last I heard, there were a few straggling women still following him. A couple of these had left their husbands to pursue the chance of fucking their way into achieving enlightenment. I am well aware that he has a nice cock, truth be told, but breaking up your family for that seems a little much. I wasn't quite that naive but I was close. Really close. So I can't exactly blame anyone for grabbing this bull by both balls. As I said, this shit is insidious.

The most fun part of all this is that I forged head on right into another cult because of it.

When word got around town about C's transgressions, another yogic "guru" was making his presence known. The alleged leader of a sect of

Sanatana Dharma, Hindu practices and duties of living a life of virtue and discipline, was appearing at another yoga studio I was affiliated with. Let's name this one F. I attended his lecture and practice one weekend and was smitten with his knack for emulating an actual spiritual Guru. Being so desperate to find a teacher who would open me up to truth and not be a sexual deviant, I thought this guy was the real deal. And true to form, he knew my latest weakness.

There were some crossovers from C to F, seeing that us wayward truth-seekers were searching for that next holy teat to suckle. His teachings were much more aligned with ancient Vedic texts. He performed pujas, a ritual involving incense, chanting and honoring the lineages of the past teachers. Oh and of course, F's picture was on the altar as well. So he must be legit! His followers were seemingly terrific people. I felt comfortable in this new gathering immediately.

Word must have gotten out about my falling out with C, given that some of his other victims were in this new magical circle. F pulled me aside after I introduced myself and off we went into some rando disciple's car to sit and talk about C and his effect on me. F didn't drive or actually take much care of himself. That, he laid upon his disciples who gathered at his "temple" (it is his house) in Omaha, Nebraska, and whomever showed up at his workshops around the country. At the time, I was impressed by his legitimacy. The flowers laid at his feet. The students kissing his feet. How everyone got to their feet when he walked into the room. Lots of feet stuff. I should have been more impressed with how much of an actual, gosh darned *cult leader* he was. Alas, he showed genuine concern for what I had been through with C and even the toxic relationship with G that I was still floating around in like numbskull detritus. He knew of C and his reputation. He vowed to help me take him down. He promised to be my true teacher. He swore he would lead the way to enlightenment.

Same Kool-Aid, different flavor. Insert that straw, Susie Q, and slurp it up.

It was really good for a while. It seemed pure. All us minions would meet up for gatherings where we sat and listened for hours to F's speeches. We meditated on candle flames, we ate meals together, we sang, we chanted mantras, we carted him around Austin in our personal cars. We ensured that his needs were cared for. When I got to sit close to him at the table of a restaurant, I was in heaven. He made me feel like a chosen one, a special soul.

Sure, there were some uncomfortable moments. For example, at one gathering, he gave me a proper finger wagging about my love of heavy metal music and horror. I was lingering too much in the darkness, he said. Others would parrot this sentiment as well. I'm just so *dark*. My response was basically that if I was so dark and bad, how did I find my way to this group? Why was I trying so hard to find the truth, find my way to "God," whatever form that may take? That shut them up. At any rate, I wasn't about to put down my metal and horror for no one.

I had shared my past sexual trauma and bat shit relationships with F. See, another opportunity for a fucking narcissist to become the overlord of my vulnerabilities. My dumb ass did it again. I eventually participated in the ritual to become one of F's official disciples. There I was, kneeling down at his feet. He placed a mala over my neck. He whispered into my ear the mantra assigned to me… Om Gam Ganapataye Namah, the mantra for Ganesh. For those of you who don't know, he's the elephant headed entity. You've seen him depicted on many young women's tattooed arms, I'm sure. Hell, I even have a Ganesh tat. I think it's mandatory for white privileged female idiots.

The best part was that, much like Kundalini, I was given a spiritual name. He said it like he had just discovered the holy grail of forced monikers. Draupadi. In the Mahabharata, the Vedic text where the Bhagavad Gita comes from, Draupadi had five husbands and was considered to be the first feminist in Hindu mythology. She would spend a year with each husband and walk through fire to reclaim her virginity before switching to the next in line. So far, pretty cool, right?

Making a long story short, Draupadi was

gambled off to some dude named Dushasana while her five husbands and male elders watched in silence. She begged the council to hear her plea that she was no one's property to be raped and taken asunder. They still did nothing. Dushasana demanded she be disrobed but when men grabbed at her sari, it kept growing back. Each time they tried, the sari grew back. They could not get her clothes off. She uncoiffed her hair and berated the men for their lack of balls and shamed them for their treatment of women. She would bring down war upon their heads for their lack of respect. Ask an Indian man in modern times and you most likely won't hear a retelling of Draupadi's story. Just like Western culture and the Bible, the rape culture of India picks and chooses which parts of the Vedic scriptures they will follow. Rape is a god-given right to some Indian men; look at the news over the past several years. Also yah, as Yogi Bhajan also decried, rape isn't a real thing.

So as much as Draupadi might be a cool name to receive, it had two major offensive flaws. First, it signified rape, which F knew was a hot button issue for me and a cause of personal trauma. Second, he blurted it out in front of the group like he was reveling in replacing my identity with that of a fictional sexual assault victim. I cried at the time because I had no fucking clue where he was going with this, and as he quickly did a Grimm's Fairy Tale version of Draup's story for the group, I was baffled and shocked that he would think this was *at all* appropriate.

That was the beginning of the end.

What clinched the exit for me was his newfound friendship with a well-known Trump supporting, scandal producing, soon to be lawsuit losing and bankrupt, former head of a hugely popular conspiracy talk show. Ok, this guy's fiancee was one of my fellow disciples. So it was an association through her; not like F went out and recruited this conservative fucktard. But this changed things. I was told by F that I'd better buy a gun and move out to the Omaha temple lest I be stuck in Austin traffic once the end times commence. Whoa boy. Some of the men in our sect swore to take up arms and be the security guard for the defense of Hinduism. Um, what? Trump was rising in popularity at the time and I was gobsmacked at how anyone could support that dickwad. Let alone my own Guru, my friends, my spiritual family.

I quietly and quickly distanced myself from this cult. I knew it was a cult by that time. My head had been painfully removed from within my ass. I had been duped yet again. It wasn't wool that I kept ripping off my unseeing eyes, several times to this point. It was a sari. A sari that refused to come off, that kept growing back. It stole my sight while everyone stood by and did nothing except wrestle with their own blinding fabric. Or perhaps some pushed it perfectly into place, a tight-fitting blindfold protecting them against the truth. The real truth.

Well after my departure from the group, one of the members contacted me out of the blue. She told me that F had roped her into a sexual relationship and was manipulating her through his knowledge of her past trauma and the fact that she was a very young single mom who was recovering from drug abuse. At first, I wasn't 100% sure if she was telling me the truth or if this was a way for F to gather information about me. From what I knew about cult leaders, her story rang true. It tracked. This man twice her age was not only leading her on, but engaging her in something she should never be forced into. I listened and, in a few subsequent phone conversations, I tried to get her to see the light. My advice fell on deaf ears. Eventually, she stopped contacting me. My guess is that it was too hard for her to process the fact that she would have to leave this thing she trusted, knew and loved for so much time. For me, it sprayed more fuel on the flame of hate I already felt toward this whole line of bullshit.

I was seeing the matrix for the first time in many years. I took the red pill. Torn out of my pod of comfort and conformity, I was horrified by the debris swirling in this high velocity funnel of reality. Debris I never wanted to capture and examine. I just let it spin. Soon enough those winds will stop and it will all come crashing down on me.

That is probably hiding in layer 245 with my rape trauma.

Burned

There's an skit on a comedy show (not saying which one so I don't get sued) where female celebrities are sitting around in a circle celebrating a well known actress' "last fuckable day." The age when a woman loses the ability to be desirable to men. The time in a woman's life that hearkens the commencement of old age. Henceforth, to all mankind, you shall be a crone, a hag, a useless shell who can offer no allure or offspring, whether wanted or not.

Of course, any sensible human who isn't a piece of shit knows that older women are still beautiful and erotic beings. Yet, there is a definitive time when we cannot biologically incubate and birth any kiddos. That much is true. It's not often spoken of, nor is it information passed along from moms to daughters, which is a damn shame.

Ah, the horrific and inevitable thing we call

menopause. Women all go through it, on a spectrum of mild to diabolical. Men seem to be completely ignorant even though they are keenly aware of our waning capacity to be considered fuckable.

This process begins with perimenopause, because why should anything be simple and quick when it comes to slipping headfirst into your ugly, chaste, feminine, unfuckable grave? It can start as early as your thirties or forties. Maybe it drags on for a decade, maybe a year. Everyone is different.

There are at least fifty symptoms associated with perimenopause (that we know of). Here are some super fun ones:

Imposter Syndrome: I'm probably not good enough to talk about this one.

Burning tongue: WTF?

Bat shit crazy: Comes on like a destructive psychotic tsunami.

Vertigo: Spin until you puke! Whee!

Weight gain around your midsection: Makes you look like a waterpark guest who got stuck inside an inner tube.

Skin that is trying to detach from your body, get really dehydrated and start the first female Antarctic death metal band whose fans all have mustaches and at least one extra long errant eyebrow hair: Still trying to come up with a good band name.

Ladies who have brain fog, memory loss, mood swings, or whatever, likely don't realize what's causing it. We take a licking and keep on ticking no matter the crippling pain and suffering du jour. As you juggle your kids and/or job and/or finances, your biology marches you right through the veil of obscurity, toward the last period, to reach your last fuckable day.

After you've endured this hormonal circus, get ready for the grande finale. Sort of. Menopause is technically just a moment in time when your reproductive organs throw in the bloody, cramping, feminine hygiene towel and cease menstruating.

Hell yeah, right? It's over!

Nope.

Depending on how much your own body hates you, postmenopause can last for more years to come. Hair grows where hair has formally feared to tread. Your vagina dries up like the Gobi, and if you're really unfuckable at this point, you'll have cobwebs.

If fucking is still within your repertoire, buy stock in lubricants, because your snatch will be keeping the KY company afloat. Heed my words, sisters. Try it dry and you'll pay. But why even do it if you cannot enjoy it?

Oh, you think it's your obligation? You have to fulfill your part of the coital deal with your partner? You don't want your significant other to run off with a younger, more vaginally moist sex bomb?

See, this is why men, especially men, need to understand the female aging process. It's not like men don't age, lose their faculties, shrink and wrinkle like inseminated abused laundry. Men should never lose their commitment while watching the fuckable drain from the one they love. Just don't coerce her arid netherlands to perform for you when she'd rather be punching holes in the drywall with her crusty knuckles during a sudden mood shift, or spinning in a forest clearing while cackling like a drunken sorceress. Don't go out and tap a young piece of strange. It's not a good look. And it's most likely dangerous for you. We get very strong during our bat shit crazy episodes.

Let's switch the roles, shall we?

You're a man who has hit his early forties. The ol' johnson ain't as responsive to visual stimuli that usually would cause stiffness that could drive nails into a 4x4. Suddenly, you can't remember where you left your tool box, issue of Sports Illustrated or gender-advantaged disparately inflated stash of disposable income. What do I know from men's possessions? You're gaining weight and break out in sobs when the wife points out your new muffin top. Your abdominal region is a steaming cesspool of radiating agony and blood flows from your pee hole area. But it's not from your pee hole. You have a third hole where your wife annoyingly wants to insert her strap-on dildo. She cannot comprehend why you don't want that at her whim, and ain't she a bitch?

You grit your teeth and succumb to her penetration as you softly weep into the pillow that she had pressed your wrinkled face into. Cries of discomfort and terror that she may notice your distended labial folds.

Look, I know men don't have that, or a third hole, but just heavily flow with this analogy, dammit.

One day she loses interest in your sudden hot flashes and bouts of ennui. The potency of your semen is that of unsweetened almond milk at this point so you're not even useful for baby making. The fact that all of this is out of control is lost on her. You are fast becoming an unfuckable man.

Maybe it's all in your head, like every non-man seems to suggest. It doesn't matter. You're confused, slightly demented and self-deprecating, but you have no idea why.

No doctor of any kind will take you or your symptoms seriously. "It's stress," they'll all say. "Just try to chill, man." Rage permeates every cell of your decrepit form as you deduce, correctly, that doctors don't care about men's health.

You get no answers. Every day is a crapshoot. What debilitating fuckery will rear its ugly head on this fine day? Migraine? Depression? Panic attacks? Constipation? Will you stop bleeding from your third hole forever or bleed every day for the next eight months until you become anemic? Your tongue is both numb and on fire. You have the fervent desire to initiate a Godzilla-level assault on your work building, yet don't have the energy to wipe your own ass.

It's only the beginning, you realize. This E-ride will only end after a decade, give or take, of this endocrine roller coaster. No one listens. No one has prepared you for this. No roadmap exists to guide you through this shit storm.

You, sir, are a man. An aging unfuckable man. Not a damn thing you can do about it. Those fucking women not only don't understand, they try to usurp your pain as if they are the ones being punished.

Men must speak out about this. Take back your power! Aging men, unite!

After all, you can't have menopause without "men."

Who Is
SUSAN SNYDER?

Susan Snyder is a two-time Splatterpunk award nominated writer of horror fiction and poetry. Her debut poetry collection, Broken Nails, was released in 2020 and was nominated for a 2021 Elgin award. Her follow up collection, Picking Scabs, was released in 2023. In 2021, Encyclopedia Sharksploitanica came out to rave reviews. A comprehensive tongue-in-cheek guide to 85 of the best and worst shark movies known to mankind, this book highlights Susan's love of self-deprecating humor and satire. Her novel collaboration with Splatterpunk award winning writer, Christine Morgan, came out in 2024.

MORE BOOKS FROM

MADNESS HEART PRESS

By Susan Snyder

- Encyclopedia Sharksploitanica
- Nympho Shark Fuck Frenzy
- Picking Scabs
- Broken Nails

By Other Authors

- Black Sunrise on Piss Earth by Charles Bernard
- The Expectant Mother's Disinformation Handbook by Robert Guffey
- Curse of the Ratman by Jay Wilburn
- Trench Mouth by Christine Morgan
- All Men Are Trash by Gina Ranalli
- The Television by Edward Lee
- A Psalm Sung in Spores by John Baltisberger
- Gush: Tales of Vaginal Horror by Gina Ranalli
- City of Spores by Austin Shirey
- Trip Chainsaw by Christian Smith
- Pure Hate by Wrath James White
- Mercy Kills by Jeff Oliver
- The Reattachment by Douglas Ford
- The Home by Judith Sonnet
- Lights Out by Nate Southard
- Kennel by Garrett Cook

www.ingramcontent.com/pod-product-compliance
Lightning Source LLC
Chambersburg PA
CBHW031217120626
46545CB00003B/882